# FIRST ENCYCLOPEDIA

W9-AAM-774

# CATS

## Contents

# What is a cat?

Cats make popular family pets. There are many different types of cat, but they all belong to a family of animals that includes big cats like lions and tigers.

Tail

## Taming cats

Domestic cats are tame animals that can be kept by people. They are all thought to be related to the Near Eastern Wildcat, which people tamed thousands of years ago.

Fur

## Cat relatives

Domestic cats are related to big cats. You can see many similarities in their behavior, including the way they sleep, move, and groom themselves.

Crossbreed Siberian

Ear

Eye

Nose

Mouth

The long, thick hairs on a cat's face are called whiskers.

## Ancient cats

Experts think that people kept cats as pets in the Middle East as early as 6,000 years ago. The Egyptians believed that all cats belonged to a goddess called Bastet. They left mummified cats in Bastet's temple to please her.

Cats' feet are called paws.

# Cat senses

All cats eat meat and have an excellent sense of sight, smell, hearing, and touch. This helps them to be successful nighttime hunters.

## Whiskers

Cats use whiskers to feel their surroundings and stop them from bumping into things. They also use whiskers to judge whether or not they can fit through small spaces.

Brown Classic Tabby

Cats can hear high-pitched sounds that we can't hear. They turn their ears around one at a time to hear sounds from all directions. This helps them to pick out their prey while hunting.

Cats have good eyesight. They can even see well in the dark.

Cats have a moist nose to smell out other animals, objects, and food.

Whisker

Whisker pad

Cats can open their jaws wide to bite their prey. They chew their food carefully before swallowing it.

# Night vision

In the wild, cats prefer to hunt just after sunset and just before sunrise. All cats, including domestic cats, have good eyesight and can see well when there is little light.

## Seeing in the dark

When it is dark, a cat opens its pupils wide to let in as much light as possible. A mirrorlike layer at the back of a cat's eye reflects light back into the eye and helps the cat to see. This is why cats' eyes glow in the dark.

Wide pupil

Pupil

In bright daylight, cats narrow their pupils to let in less light.

## Shapes and colors

Cats' eyes come in a variety of shapes and colors depending on their breed. Most Siamese cats have blue slanted eyes, while most longhair and shorthair cats have green, amber, or blue rounded eyes.

# Paws, claws, and tails

With sharp claws and a long tail, most cats are skilled at hunting, balancing, and squeezing through tight spaces. Their tails help them to balance, while sharp claws allow them to scratch and dig things.

There are over 20 bones in a cat's tail, which makes it very bendable. Most cats have tails, but some Manx cats have no tail at all.

## Claws

Cats push their claws in and out of folds of skin, called sheaths, in their paws. When they are walking, they keep their claws in. This stops the claws from getting blunt too quickly. To sharpen their claws, cats scratch things like tree trunks and furniture.

## Silent stalker

Underneath a cat's paw is a soft pad that helps the cat to walk quietly.

Cats walk by bringing each paw around in front of the other. This means they can easily balance as they walk along branches and fences.

Cats can feel vibrations on the ground through their paws. This lets them know that someone else is nearby.

Cats walk on their toes.

# Fur

Cats' fur keeps them warm and helps to protect their skin. Different breeds of cat have different types of fur. Most cats have short hair, but some cats that originally came from very cold countries have longer, thicker hair.

Short-haired cat ——→

Blue Point Siamese

## "Hairless" cats

Sphynx cats look like they don't have any fur. Some do in fact have a little hair, but it is hard for them to keep themselves warm.

## Grooming

When cats clean themselves, the hairs that they swallow can form hair balls in their stomach. To prevent this, many people groom their cats with brushes and combs. Grooming also prevents the fur of long-haired cats from becoming knotted and matted.

## Shedding fur

Cats grow more fur in winter so that they have a thicker, winter coat to keep them warm. Their hair also falls out throughout the year. This is called shedding. Cats shed most fur in the spring as they get rid of their winter coat.

Long-haired cat

Domestic Longhair

# Coats and colors

Each different kind of domestic cat is called a breed. Most people have short-haired cats that are a mixture of breeds. These cats are called moggies. Other cats have been bred to have certain features or look a particular way.

Devon Rex

## Cat colors

Cats' fur can come in many different colors.

Red

Black

Blue

White

Chocolate

Lilac

Cream

People are able to breed cats to make sure that their coat is a certain color or pattern.

Tortoiseshell coats can be a mixture of black, red, and cream. Almost all tortoisehell cats are female.

Spotted

Tortoiseshell

Tabby

Many wild cats also have a tabby coat, which helps them to blend in with the background and hide.

Pointed

Blue-Cream

# Different cats

There are three main groups of short-haired cats: British shorthairs, American shorthairs, and Oriental shorthairs.

## British shorthair cats

British shorthairs are short, stocky cats with round eyes, a round head, and strong legs.

British Shorthair (Blue)

## American shorthair cats

American shorthairs are large, broad cats, making them strong hunters.

American Shorthair (Tabby)

# Oriental shorthair cats

Oriental shorthairs have slim bodies and like attention. Siamese cats in particular will meow all day to their owners, other cats, and themselves!

Siamese (Pointed)

Abyssinian
(Tabby and White)

Bengal (Spotted)

# Longhair cats

Many long-haired cats require daily combing to prevent their fur from matting.

Persian

Turkish Angora

Maine Coon

# Cats in action

In the wild, cats use all their senses to hunt and catch their prey. Domestic cats are fed by their owners, but they still hunt and catch animals like mice, rats, frogs, and birds. Most domestic cats hunt for fun.

## Falling

If a cat falls from a height, it will almost always land on its feet. As it falls, the cat twists it head and legs around and then arches its back to help it land gently on the ground.

## Crouching

When a cat sees or hears its prey, it crouches down and then creeps slowly and quietly towards the prey. The cat will then silently watch with its ears and whiskers pointing forwards.

# Jumping

Cats can jump to catch their prey. They are good jumpers and can reach heights that are over five times the height of their body.

# Climbing

Cats like to climb. They hold on to trees and branches with their claws.

# Pouncing

Before pouncing on its prey, a cat may wiggle its bottom! When it is ready, the cat quickly jumps forward with its claws out of their sheaths, set to catch the prey.

# Keeping clean

Cats like to keep clean and can spend a long time licking themselves, using their rough tongue to remove dirt and knots in their fur.

A cat can twist its neck so it can reach all of its body.

Cats lick their paws and then use them to wipe their face as if with a washcloth.

If a cat's paws become sticky, it will clean them immediately by spreading out each paw and pulling out any dirt with its tongue.

## Tough tongue

The cat's tongue is tough and spiny. Cats use their rough tongue like a comb to groom their fur.

Cats clean their belly to make the fur straight and comfortable.

## Scent spreading

By keeping clean and licking their whole body, cats spread their personal scent all around their body. By rubbing against trees and other objects, cats spread their scent further for other cats and animals to pick up.

# Cat naps

Sleeping is a very important part of a cat's day. In the wild, cats hunt at night, so they naturally sleep during the day. Domestic cats will sleep at night and throughout the day – they can spend up to 18 hours a day napping!

Cats may keep one eye a little bit open to check for any danger.

When it's cold, cats look for somewhere warm to sleep. They will also curl up and put their face between their paws to keep the heat in.

Newborn kittens spend even more time sleeping than adult cats. In the wild, this would help to keep them out of trouble, by preventing them from wandering off and being seen or heard by predators.

When it's hot, cats pick high, shady places to sleep, or lie stretched out to keep cool.

# Cats and kittens

Baby domestic cats are called kittens. A female cat usually has between two and five kittens, but she can have as many as ten and they can all be different colors. A family of kittens is called a litter. Wild cats' babies are often called cubs instead of kittens.

Kittens feed on their mother's milk by sucking on a teat. After about three weeks, they are ready to eat solid food.

## Playtime

Kittens love to play with toys and with each other. When they play-fight with other kittens, it may look aggressive, but they won't hurt each other! By creeping up on things and chasing toys, kittens learn how to hunt through play.

Mother cats teach their kittens how to clean themselves.

Scottish Fold

## First sight

Newborn kittens are blind for the first nine days of their life. Once open, their eyes are usually blue but may then change to green or amber.

# Cat chat

Cats can tell you how they feel by the noises they make, the way that they move their ears, and the way that they change their eyes.

## Cross

If a cat is cross, it will hiss, growl, flatten its ears, and flick its tail from side to side.

## Affectionate

Cats will rub against a person's legs to show them affection. In doing so, they also rub their scent on to the person.

## Feeling safe

If a cat rolls on its back and shows its belly, it may be telling you that it trusts you and feels safe, or it may be defending itself.

## Frightened

When cats are frightened, they flatten their ears, and fluff up their fur so that they look bigger.

## Happy

Cats make a deep noise in their throat when they are happy. This noise is called purring.

# Cat tails

Cats can also show you that they are happy or upset through their tails.

## Happy

If a cat sits with its tail wrapped around its body, it shows that it is happy.

When a cat is happy or pleased to see you, it will put its tail straight up and point its ears forwards. It may also greet you with a meow and arch its back.

28

## Defensive

If a cat's tail hangs down, it may mean the cat is feeling defensive or aggressive.

## Nervous

When a cat's tail trembles, it may be feeling nervous. If the cat begins to flick its tail aggressively or thump it from side to side while it is sitting, it may mean that the cat is feeling angry and annoyed.

# Glossary

This glossary explains some of the harder words in the book.

**breed** A particular type or kind of animal.

**creep** To move slowly and carefully in order not to be seen or heard.

**crouch** When an animal or person bends their legs to be close to the ground.

**cub** The young of certain wild animals, including tigers, lions, foxes, and bears.

**domestic** A domestic animal is one that can be kept as a pet. Domestic animals are not dangerous, nor are they scared of people.

**eyesight** The ability to see.

**groom** To brush and clean the coat of an animal.

**growl** To make a deep, rumbling sound, often to show anger.

**hair ball** A ball of hair that builds up in a cat's stomach as a result of the cat cleaning itself.

**hunter** An animal that looks for and kills another animal for food.

**kitten** A baby domestic cat.

**litter** A group of kittens or other young animals born to a mother animal at one time.

**matted** Hair that is tangled up in a thick clump.

**pounce** To jump suddenly in order to grab or take something.

**prey** An animal that is hunted and eaten by another animal.

**pupil** A dark, circular opening in the center of the eye. The pupil changes shape to let more or less light into the eye.

**purr** To make a soft, low, rumbling sound. Cats purr when they are happy.

**scent** A smell.

**sheath** The folds of skin on a cat's paw that protect and hold its claws.

**shedding** When a cat loses its hair. After shedding its hair, a cat grows back a new coat.

**stocky** Something that is short and sturdy.